SAVE THE BLACK MAN

Blessings In Disguise

Written by
Lewis Burt

This book may be purchased in bulk for educational, business, or sales promotional use.

© 2022 by Words of Wisdom Publishing.
Published in Pittsburg, PA.
Book Design by Ashley Mae Pancho.
Illustrated by Ashley Mae Pancho.

ISBN (Paperback): 979-8-9857424-2-8
ISBN (Ebook): 979-8-9857424-3-5
Library of Congress Control Number (LCCN): 2022904743

Follow Lewis Burt on social media:

Twitter: @RealMrBurt
Instagram: @RealMrBurt
Facebook: @RealMrBurt

CONTENT

DEDICATION

THIS BOOK IS dedicated to everyone who has experienced, those who are currently experiencing, and those who will experience some form of adversity in their lifetime.

Remember that you are resilient; your life has value and purpose regardless of what you may be experiencing at the moment. Please remain hopeful and remember that you are loved.

Acknowledgments

FIRST AND FOREMOST, I must acknowledge God for using me as a vessel. Thank you, Lord, for opening my spiritual eyes and ears. Because of you, I feel purposeful.

Secondly, I would like to thank Robert Nelson, Kathleen Cesare, and Dr. Sharon Kotch for giving me motivation to put my pen to paper and write my story.

I also want to thank big Stacks. Rest with God, big brother; this is for you, and for our culture.

Lastly, I want to thank my mother for always being my rock. Thank you!

ABOUT THE AUTHOR

BORN AND RAISED in Pittsburgh, Pennsylvania, Lewis Burt III birthed his first novel behind a barbed wire fence using a pad and pen to write through his experiences.

"*Save the Black Man*" is a mirror into the heart and soul of Lewis—reflecting love, defeat, pain, maturity, and hope.

PREFACE

I HAVE FOUND an innovative way to not only tell my story of saving the Black man, but also to offer my story as a guide to help readers overcome adversity through faith and spiritual growth. I know that what I experienced is much bigger than me, so I am compelled to share the lessons that I learned throughout the most painful moments of my life. You will find that each entry in this book offers a title, quote, personal story, lesson, and a way to move forward.

INTRODUCTION

Every morning when I open my eyes, I thank God for a new day.
My story is still being written, and today I'm on a new page.

I made a lot of poor choices in my life, and it took years for me to learn that if I keep playing with fire...I'm going to keep getting burned.

I'm grateful for my prison sentence, because I was blind, but now I see.

I know that sounds crazy, but my punishment was key.

It was the key to unlock change so I could start thinking rationally.
I need to do what's right because I know what's right...and not because somebody asked me.

Excuses are a lifeline and just another reason why you can't.
Stay focused, be confident, and tell yourself that you can!

I haven't seen it all, but trust me...I've seen a lot.
I'm going to lead by example: please follow me to the top.

> *Proverbs 14:16 | The wise are cautious and avoid danger; fools plunge ahead with reckless confidence.*

RECKLESS

MAY 5TH OF 2014 was a day I can honestly say that God spared my life. I can still remember it vividly: it was an early spring morning, and I was on my way to drop off narcotics to one of my customers. As I got closer to my destination, I noticed a couple of plainclothes detectives in an unmarked Subaru staking out the premises. At that point, I tried to elude the officers by driving past my original destination. The unmarked vehicle immediately did a U-turn and was now behind me in pursuit of a high-speed chase. After running countless stop signs and traffic lights, I abandoned my vehicle and continued to flee on foot. I was now running through Greenfield—a suburban neighborhood in Pittsburgh, Pennsylvania—with a bag full of narcotics in my left hand, and a .40 caliber handgun in my right hand.

My super-optimism fooled me into believing that I was about to get away...and that's when it hit me: I felt a paralyzing sensation from the officer's taser gun. Falling to the ground, face first, I instantly tasted blood in my mouth due to the impact from hitting the pavement. I remember the officer flipping me over and prying the firearm out of my hand. After he cuffed me, he started punching me in my face, and then the officer whispered in my ear and said, "Killing you would've been awesome."

Two weeks after that particular incident, I was federally indicted on a heroin drug conspiracy. After six years of running #Reckless in the streets, I was once again back in prison. Now that I was forced to sit still in a cell without any drugs or alcohol to cloud my mind, I was finally able to see how irrational my behavior was.

I also remember right around that time how I would come out of my cell early in the morning to watch CNN. A young man named Michael Brown had just been shot and killed by a police officer in Ferguson, Missouri. When I saw what happened to Michael Brown, as I watched the news, I felt sick to my stomach. I just kept hearing that officer whispering in my ear and telling me, "Killing you would've been awesome." Even though I believe his comments were inappropriate, my heart tells me that my actions on that day could've easily cost me my life...and sadly, I can't say that him shooting me wouldn't have been justifiable. As careless, #Reckless, and just plain stupid as I was, that officer chose to use his taser gun instead of live rounds.

Recently, I've been reflecting on my #Reckless behavior, and I was able to identify why I would constantly put myself in high risk situations. The three C's opened my eyes and allowed me to shed light on some things that I probably never would've discovered without this program. I learned that no matter how bad the neighborhood was, or how hard things got, I always had a choice to do what was right...or what was wrong.

My problem was that I would constantly allow my cognitions to control my mind state. I struggled with making excuses to justify my actions; I also struggled to have any internal motivation within myself. For years, I chose crime because I wasn't ready to change. Looking back and realizing how much time I've lost in my life makes me feel deflated and set back.

I challenge myself by understanding that my life is only going to be what I make it. If I work hard and bust my tail for an honest living and leave my criminal lifestyle in my rearview, the sky's the limit. If I choose to keep struggling with super-optimism—thinking that I can get away with a life of crime—then my life is already over.

Moving forward, I will continue to challenge my irrational beliefs when I find myself thinking about the criminal lifestyle. I will also recall the countless days I've spent in prison as a reminder of where I never want to be again, once I'm free. Most importantly, I will make it a priority to change my people, places, and things, because I now realize that a fresh start is the best start.

THE THREE C'S LIFESTYLE THEORY

CONDITIONS: Characteristics of the individual, or one's environmental situation which serves to either increase or decrease risk for future criminal involvement.

CHOICE: Decision making process whereby the individual selects one or more options in dealing with various situations, problems, and events.

COGNITIONS: A style of thinking designed to justify, support, and maintain one's thinking and evolving criminal lifestyle.

> *Martin Luther King, Jr. | I have a dream that my four little children will one day live in a nation where they will be judged on the content of their character.*

DREAMS

I STILL REMEMBER when I was in elementary school and my first grade teacher Mrs. Cole asked me what I wanted to be when I grew up. As a child I used to #Dream of being an NFL superstar. Every time I would see the players on the TV screen, I would daydream about how amazing it would be to wear one of those jerseys while having millions of fans chanting my name.

The thing I've learned about having a #Dream is that #Dreams are free. #Dreams are a part of our fantasies, and only we have the power to turn them into reality.

Looking back, although football was something that I loved and was very passionate about, when the time came for me to capture the moment, my priorities were not where they needed to be. Instead, I began to focus on criminal activity. I became so tangled up in my own web of discontinuity that without notice, my whole mindset changed, and I was now knee-deep into a life of crime.

Recently, I was thinking about the goals I set for myself to accomplish in the next five years, and this had me pondering my release back into society. I started considering some of the roadblocks that were going to be in my path—just thinking about them had me concerned and feeling uncertain about my future. I was struggling to find a solution on how I was going to get around those barriers.

I found myself asking for advice from an older inmate from Baltimore, Maryland, who I respected highly. His wisdom, knowledge, and experience were enough to help me challenge my worries, and I was able to find a sense of peace.

Moving forward, no matter what, I will stay focused on my short- and long-term goals. I will follow my intuition and remain ambitious about my future. I will also constantly remind myself that a goal without a plan is just a #Dream.

> *Serenity Prayer | God grants me the serenity to accept the things I cannot change, the courage to change the things I can, and the wisdom to know the difference.*

WAITING ON MY MOMENT

SOMETIMES IN LIFE we experience moments that become engraved in our memories—moments that no matter how hard we try to forget, we just can't. A few particular moments I can't seem to shake involve me becoming a statistic of recidivism. For example, 111-963, GG-8877, and 35321-068 are three different prisoner numbers that were used to identify me as an inmate in the county, state, and in the feds.

Every time I came to prison, I found myself being traumatized with a routine that became all too familiar to me. Getting fingerprinted and strip-searched left me feeling violated and uncivilized. When that cell door would slam shut, reality would set in, and I would analyze the bruises that were left on my wrists (from the handcuffs being so tight).

Each time I returned to prison, the only way to truly describe my experience was...déjà vu.

While recently reflecting on my life, I was ashamed that I spent so many valuable years locked behind these walls. Every time I think about my future plans and goals, I feel deflated and setback because I still feel like I'm stuck at a standstill. I constantly ask myself, "Where would you be if you would have just gone to school and landed a career a long time ago?" I answer myself by saying, "Not here at F.C.I. Fort Dix."

I struggle with waking up in prison each day and forcing myself to become accustomed to a lifestyle that I'm not proud of. I struggle with eating the food they serve. I struggle with having a flashlight shined in my face while I'm sleeping. I struggle with having a long distance relationship with my children.

Every time I left prison, I would always say to myself, "I'm never coming back to jail again!" I would say that I wasn't coming back because I didn't think that I would get caught again.

Somewhere in my mind, I actually thought that prison made me smarter. My thought process was that I would just keep a low profile and be more careful the next time. That was my super-optimism talking, and that's why I am exactly where I am in my life today.

A wise man once told me that time and experience are the best teachers in life. This I believe to be true, because today I'm just tired of being sick and tired.

I honestly believe that I'll be able to challenge my criminal thinking patterns once I'm released from prison because, internally, I'm ready to change. I'm ready to put my thoughts into action and prove to myself that I can be a better son, father, and productive member of society. I'm ready to challenge myself by simply doing what's right for a change.

Moving forward, I will continue to wait patiently on #MyMoment. I'm waiting for the moment when I can help my mother with her grocery shopping like I used to, or the moment when I can finally hold my children in my arms after being separated from them for so many years.

I constantly have dreams of my own white picket fence, and living happily ever after...even if it's only for a moment.

RECIDIVISM

DO YOU KNOW what recidivism is? It's the tendency for a convicted criminal to reoffend. Recidivism is the act of a person repeating an undesirable behavior after they have either experienced negative consequences of that behavior, or after they have been trained to extinguish that behavior. It is also used to refer to the percentage of former prisoners who are rearrested for a similar offense.

The cause of recidivism is complex and likely due to a combination of personal, sociological, economic, and lifestyle factors. Common explanations for recidivism include elements within the criminal justice system that might make someone more likely to engage in criminal behavior again.

The U.S. releases over seven million people from jail and more than six-hundred thousand people from prison each year. Recidivism is common. Within three years of their release, two out of three people are rearrested, and more than 50% are incarcerated again.

There's an imaginary line that I can't see: will I cross it?
I just got my freedom back and look how quick I've lost it.

I knew that I was struggling but I couldn't see my blind spots.
I didn't challenge anything; I got tripped up by the roadblocks.

Now I'm back in handcuffs; look how fast it happened.
I said I was going to change, but I didn't show it through my actions.

In and out of jail...I can hear my family's voices.
"You ain't never going to change! You're still making poor choices!"

Now I feel powerless because I can't see my future.
I can only blame myself, and I'm just being truthful.

If prison is not where I want to spend my life feeling like I'm shackled up in chains,
I need to confront the man in the mirror, and tell him it's time for him to change.

Psalms 119:105 | Your word is a lamp to my feet and light to my path.

NEW YEARS

FOR AS LONG AS I can remember, every New Year's Eve I would always set a new goal. I would try to choose a new goal that I thought would make my life better—I'm a fan of having a new year's resolution.

Each year, motivating myself to change for the better has always been powerful, and something I've become accustomed to, so on December 31, I always celebrate a new me.

Recently, I was thinking about all of the valuable years I've spent in the penal system. When I started adding up the numbers in my head, I felt sick at heart...and ashamed.

Thinking about where I could've been in my life versus where I'm at right now is demoralizing. I struggle everyday with the thought of, "Damn, did I just let life pass me by?" I also struggle with thinking that I can make up for lost time.

Each day that I'm stuck behind these walls is a day that I'll never get back, and this pains me. I challenge myself every day by placing all of my worries in God's hands.

I also challenge myself by believing that my present term of incarceration is my blessing in disguise. These valuable years lost from my life have really opened my eyes, and I came to realize that these years don't have to be lost.

Growing as a person and finding peace in my mind has allowed me to see life more clearly, so instead of stressing and complaining, I've learned to adapt and evolve.

Moving forward, I will look past the barbed wire fence that surrounds me. When I open my eyes, I will imagine and believe that I'm a student attending Morehouse College. Finally, with my tuition paid in full, I will take the opportunity to educate myself because knowledge—plus wisdom—equals understanding.

Bedtime Prayer | Now I lay myself down to sleep. I pray to the Lord for my soul to keep. If I should die before I wake, I pray to the Lord my soul to take. Amen.

DREAMS AND NIGHTMARES

I STILL REMEMBER my daughter Kyra's first day of school. It was one of those special moments that every father #Dreams of—this was a moment I'd been dreaming of since the day my daughter was born. With butterflies in my stomach, I woke up so excited like it was my first day of school.

While my daughter Kyra and I sat at the kitchen table eating Fruity Pebbles, I asked her if she was nervous. She responded by saying, "Yes, I'm scared Dad!" and then she asked me if I could come to school with her and stay for the entire day.

I told her, "Daddy can't go to school with you, but I promise that I'll be waiting for you as soon as you get off the school bus with your favorite ice cream."

When I said, "ice cream," she flashed me her beautiful smile, and that's when I woke up in another cold sweat. Damn! It was another bad dream. Here I was still at F.C.I. Fort Dix having the same painful #Nightmare about missing my daughter's first day of school.

Just recently, I opened my locker and BOOM! there it was, staring me in the face: the picture of my daughter Kyra with her pink shirt, shoes, and book bag on her first day of school.

Every time I stare at that picture, I can't help but to smile...but the day that picture was taken is a day that still haunts me.

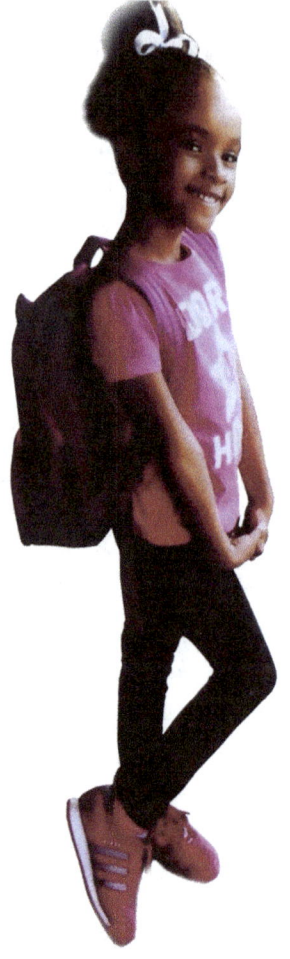

I struggle with this tremendously because I know I missed one of those precious moments in my daughter's life that I'll never be able to get back. I also struggle with constantly beating myself up as a father and this often leads me to feel inadequate.

Each day I wake up on the other side of this fence is another day that I can't physically be a father, and this makes me feel powerless. I will challenge myself first by continuing to be the best father that I can be from my current position. I will also challenge myself by trying my best to let go of my self-defeating thoughts because I know I can't change the past. The most important challenge for me is to go home and stay home because I truly understand how my selfish actions have victimized my own children.

Moving forward, I'm truly grateful that I will still have the opportunity to be present for many more accomplishments and precious milestones in my children's lives. I will also use my present term of incarceration as a wakeup call, because even with all my past failures as a father, my children still love me dearly and view me as their superhero.

Lastly, I will continue to have sweet #Dreams about the day when I can reunite with my children and (hopefully, sooner than later) when I open my eyes, this #Nightmare will finally be over.

> *Isaiah 43:2 | When you go through deep waters, I will be with you.*

TRIALS AND TRIBULATIONS

WHEN I THINK ABOUT #TrialsAndTribulations, the first thing that comes to mind is my son—his name is Josiah Burt and when he was just six months old, he was diagnosed with Wilms tumor. Wilms tumor (also called nephroblastoma) is a rare form of cancer that attacks the kidneys and is typically found in young children.

When a child is born they are so fragile, innocent, and full of life. To watch Josiah battle against something so deadly at a young age was heartbreaking, and tearful. I'll never forget his chemotherapy process. It's one thing to see a stranger (or even a person on TV) lose their hair to cancer, but to witness it happening to my son was unbearable. I felt like I was watching him burn in red hot flames and there was nothing I could do to put the fire out.

Cancer is a disease caused by an uncontrolled division of abnormal cells in the part of the body. A cancer is also something evil or destructive that is hard to contain or destroy. To hear the doctor say that my son was now cancer-free—after five long years of not knowing if the cancer would return—was one of the greatest moments of my life.

Josiah didn't know that he had cancer at the time, because his mother and I agreed not to tell him. We figured, why stress our son out with painful news about him possibly dying? Instead, we felt as if Josiah should wake up like all normal kids: with no worries.

As parents, we kept that secret from our son to protect his sanity. Josiah has been granted one wish of anything he desires from the Make-A-Wish Foundation; he will be turning thirteen in August, and still hasn't decided to make his wish!

Recently, I was talking to him on the jail phone, and I expressed how proud he makes me feel as his father. Josiah is an honor roll student, and he also plays for two basketball leagues, despite having one kidney. During my incarceration, Josiah has blossomed into the young man that I had dreams of him becoming.

I struggle with not being present for his transformation from boy to young man. I also struggle with the example that I'm currently setting by sitting in this six-by-eight jail cell.

I'm going to challenge myself first by understanding that my son still loves me, despite my failures as his father. Next, I will challenge myself by becoming a better man for my son to follow, because I'll be damned if I lead him to a jail cell!

Moving forward, I will continue to work on myself daily because I understand that my son will ultimately follow in my footsteps. I will also take this opportunity to keep climbing the ladder of hope. Lastly when I reach the top of that ladder I will stop and reminisce—even if only for a moment—about my past #TrialsAndTribulations.

STATISTICS OF FATHERLESS CHILDREN IN AMERICA

CHILDREN WHO GROW UP in fatherless homes have a greater risk of major challenges in life than those who grow up with a father at home. We might want to believe otherwise, and there are many children who overcome the hardships associated with an absent father, but the truth is in the data.

According to the Annie E. Casey Foundation's website, National Kids Count, approximately 35% of children under the age of eighteen live in a single parent home as of 2016. As many as 25% of children in the U.S. live in a household with a mother alone—that is over eighteen million children who do not live with a father figure.

Additionally, father-only households were noted at just 8%. Statistics show that women-only households are more likely to live below the poverty line. In 2016, the U.S. Census Bureau reported that these types of families increased to 28%—this leaves children vulnerable to a variety of social hardships throughout their lives.

The American Academy of Pediatrics (AAP) notes that one in five children (more than 40%) in the U.S. fall into this category of poor or "near-poor." While this includes families with two parents as well, the study shows the disadvantages these children face.

African Proverb | The child who is not embraced by the village will burn it down to feel its warmth.

TO TAKE FOR GRANTED

EVERY DAY at some point or another, I find myself in deep thought about how I took my freedom for granted. My situational awareness was practically non-existent! Even though I knew my irrational behavior could have consequences, I never really thought long and hard about the ripple effects of my actions.

Now, every time I talk to my eight-year-old daughter, she asks me when I'm coming home from prison. Each time she asks, the only response I have enough courage to give her is, "I'll be home soon." Knowing how much she needs me, and not being able to be there for my daughter, tears me apart.

As the years come and go, I've noticed how much my absence has deeply affected my children. I came to understand that even though I'm the one physically serving this prison sentence, my absence has caused pain and despair to the people I love the most. The time given to me by the judge was supposed to be received as a punishment, but I've been using this experience to become a better father for my children.

Recently, I caught myself daydreaming about having my freedom restored. I started pondering about what I was going to do on my first day out of prison—popping up and surprising my children was at the top of my list. Just thinking about their reaction brought a smile to my face and warmth to my heart. I've been struggling with becoming accustomed to the long distance relationship that I have with my children. Missing birthdays, graduations, and first days of school has been extremely painful.

With every day that comes and goes, more and more precious moments slip through my fingers, and I'm beginning to feel inadequate. I'm learning to challenge my self-defeating thoughts by understanding that I've made some poor choices in my life. I also realize that dwelling in self-pity isn't going to get me anywhere.

Moving forward, I will not dwell on the past because there's nothing I can do to change it. I will stay focused by concentrating on the present and the future. Lastly, I will be more mindful not #ToTakeForGranted how my selfish actions can—and will—affect others.

Proverbs 30:17 | The eye that mocks a father and scorns to obey a mother will be picked out by the ravens of the valley and eaten by the vultures.

Save The Black Man

FATHER

WHEN I THINK about my #Father, to be honest, my emotions are numb.

I recall meeting him for the first time in my life when I was twelve years old. I remember staring him in the face all while saying to myself, "Who are you? You don't love me. You're not my Dad!"

For years I was waiting to meet the man who gave me his name and signed my birth certificate. When I stared at him, I felt disturbed and abandoned because I saw a reflection of me in him. For so many years I couldn't wait to meet my #Father, but at that moment I wished it never happened.

Recently, I was analyzing myself as a #Father and to be honest, I'm ashamed of who I've become. Being incarcerated has physically taken me out of my children's lives. Having a long distance relationship with my children has been traumatizing, to say the least. Many days they have cried to me while on our jail phone calls; as their #Father, not being able to walk through the door and wipe away their tears makes me feel pained, and worthless.

I constantly struggle with being honest to my children about when I'm being released from prison because I don't think they can handle the truth. I struggle with the guilt of abandoning my children just like my #Father abandoned me. This makes me feel like a hypocrite because I'm now causing my children the same pain I experienced as a child.

I'm going to challenge myself first by trying to find forgiveness in my heart for my #Father because time and experience has taught me that no one is perfect. I will also challenge myself by setting realistic goals that will put me in a position to be a better #Father for my children.

Today I came to understand that money could never buy me happiness. I'd rather be broke and with my children everyday versus being wealthy and confined to a cell. These years spent away from my children have been sorrowful and I never want to disappoint them again!

Moving forward, I will continue to be the best #Father that I can be from my current position. Each day I will strive to be a better me for my children, and for myself.

I will make it a priority to be and stay in their lives forever.

> *Proverbs 15:3 | The eyes of the Lord are in every place keeping watch on the evil, and the good.*

SKELETONS IN MY CLOSET

EVERYBODY has at least one secret. You know, that secret that you promise to take to the grave? The one that you keep to yourself because you can't fathom the thought of other people judging you on your truth? These are some of my untold secrets...or should I say, I have a few skeletons that I've kept in my closet.

Several months ago, I received some horrible news about my uncle passing away. His name was Marcus McClung, and he was my favorite uncle. He was found dead in an abandoned house in Homewood, an east side neighborhood in Pittsburgh. When the coroners found his body, I was told that he died cold, stiff, and alone, with a heroin needle stuck in his arm.

When I started to think about the memories that we shared together, the one that stood out the most was the last time I saw my uncle Marcus alive—the last time I saw him alive, I sold him some heroin. To be honest, I had sold my uncle Marcus heroin on many different occasions. I know I'm not responsible for my uncle Marcus's death, but I do feel guilty and ashamed knowing that he did ultimately die from the same poison that I had sold to him and countless others.

Another skeleton that I must remove from my closet is one that I've been holding on to for way too long. When I was nine years old, I witnessed my stepfather beat and rape my mother. I was so traumatized and in disbelief that I didn't actually accept what happened until I was in my twenties. This is the first time that I've ever disclosed this...and I don't know why I've held this in for so many years. Is it because I was ashamed? Maybe it was too hard for me to talk about...or is it because I struggle with using the cut-off and bottling up my emotions?

Recently, I was on the phone having a conversation with my son. My son just turned thirteen, and I felt like it was time for me to be direct and assertive with him about some of the #SkeletonsInMyCloset. I disclosed that when I was his age, I started making poor choices by using and selling drugs. I also made my son aware of my current charges: heroin distribution and firearm possession. I stated that if he ever ended up in prison, I'd feel like I failed as his father.

I struggle with the thought of even imagining my son having handcuffs locked around his wrist. I also struggle with being a father behind these walls because I feel like it's impossible to lead by example when I'm trying to preach through collect calls. This makes me feel dishonored and powerless, and I pray every night that I can fill that void for all the years I've been absent as his father.

I will challenge myself first by having an honest conversation with my son, and I will be willing to answer any questions he may have. I will also learn to disclose things that seem impossible to talk about, because I now understand that if I continue to keep these #SkeletonsInMyCloset, I'm only suppressing the pain, guilt, and anger that continues to kill me inside.

Moving forward, I'd be lying if I said I was going to be more open with people about my deepest, darkest secrets. What I can say is, I will try to find someone I can trust—someone who won't judge me about things that are uncomfortable for me to talk about. I came to understand that no one is perfect, and that we are all apprehensive and hesitant to share a piece of ourselves that makes us feel vulnerable. With this in mind, I will strive to eventually clean out my closet full of bones.

FROM ME TO YOU

TODAY, a huge problem in the Black community is the way we tend to think. The statistics show that we are continuing to make poor choices at an alarming rate. We're dropping out of school, filling up prison cells, and we're leaving our children fatherless. I know because I personally helped to contribute to all three categories.

My name is Lewis Burt III. I am a Black man. I've made some poor choices in my life. I know that I have to do better for myself, and for Black men in general. I've learned in life that no matter how bad the circumstances may seem, we always have the option to do what's wrong or what's right.

NO OTHER OPTION

In the past, I didn't think I had an option.

My rent was overdue, and I had to make a profit.

I chose to get it poppin'.

Worst decision of my life: once I started selling drugs, I couldn't stop it.

Now, I gotta stay cautious.

Firearm on my waist because it's real, and I ain't trying to see a coffin.

There is no other option.

My habitat feels like a jungle; my ribs are touching, and I'm starving.

My kids need their father.

If I die, or go to jail will they prevail? Will they ever go to college?

Will they have an option?

Will my son try to follow in my footsteps, and inherit all my problems?

I'm labeled as a convict.

I was found guilty of a criminal offense; I couldn't stay away from nonsense.

Now, I'm in the process of trying to get my freedom back. It's been a long, tough road. I'm exhausted.

Recently I've switched plans.

I'm trying to change my whole life; I don't want to die in prison as an old man.

I'm struggling! I'm struggling!

If I come home and I can't find a job, will I turn back to hustling?

Never said that I was perfect here...I said I'm struggling!

I need honest feedback: somebody come and help me here.

I just want to raise my kids and get my life together.

I have to challenge this. The clock is ticking: now or never.

I don't want to end up back.

I'm going to constantly remember where I came from—that's how I'll challenge that.

Moving forward, what's my goal?

I'm changing my people, places, and things. Everything's new, nothing old.

There's no other option.

That's a roadblock, because in the end, everybody has an option.

Only I can make my choice.

I'm going to always let my conscience be my guide, and follow that little voice.

I have options!

> *Proverbs 31:26 | She opens her mouth with wisdom, and the teaching of kindness is on her tongue.*

IN MY MOTHER'S WORDS

THE LAST TIME I saw my son Lewis was the day I went to watch him get sentenced in a federal courtroom. I'll never forget the bright orange jumpsuit he was wearing as he stood there shackled in chains from his wrists, down to his ankles.

As a #Mother, watching my son in that courtroom right before he lost valuable years from his life was heartbreaking, and extremely painful. As the marshals walked my son out of the courtroom, my son made eye contact with me. I gave him my #Motherly smile, with tearful eyes. My son smiled back and said to me, "Stop crying!"

Over the past couple of years, we've only been able to communicate through letters and jail phone calls. Every time I talk to my son Lewis on the phone, he always seems to be in good spirits. My son tells me that he's programming, and also setting realistic goals that he'll be able to tackle upon his release from prison.

As a #Mother, I just want to see all my children free, and in a position to fend for themselves if something was to ever happen to me. I have six children, and my three sons are all currently in prison. Many nights I've watched the news and just shook my head in disgust at the senseless gun violence that takes place in the city of Pittsburgh. Even though I miss all three of my sons, sometimes I say to myself, "At least I know they're alive in prison."

Recently, I've been thinking about my youngest son's release back into society. My youngest son was recently shot in his chest, and then he was arrested for having illegal possession of a firearm less than two weeks after he was released from the hospital. I worry about him picking up where he left off when he comes home. I ask myself, "Will my son seek revenge, or just listen to his #Mother and let it go?"

I constantly struggle with feeling powerless about not having enough influence to discourage my three sons from participating in criminal activities. I struggle with my three sons becoming victims of the penal system, but I struggle most with the thought of losing one of my children for good.

I challenge myself everyday by being the best #Mother that I can be for all my children. I also challenge myself by placing my worries in God's hands.

God, please wrap your wings around my children and keep them safe from the dangers of this cold world.

Every day is a challenge when raising children, but as a #Mother, this is something that I've become accustomed to. Moving forward, I will continue to use my #Motherly instinct and my intuition to guide my children towards a life of love, happiness, and success.

I will make it my duty to be there even in their darkest moments of guilt, shame, and regret. Lastly, no matter what may happen in this lifetime, my friendship, my loyalty, and love will never change because #Mommy loves her babies.

RESENTMENT

DO YOU KNOW what resentment is? #Resentment is the process of dwelling on a painful or upsetting situation to the point that it causes you anger and bitterness. #Resentment can eat away at you and poison your heart against trusting others, feeling compassion, or being open to love in the future.

You can release #Resentment in five steps:

(1) ACKNOWLEDGE #Resentment. Since the process always starts with being honest with yourself, the first step to releasing #Resentment is to acknowledge that you feel resentful.

(2) IDENTIFY where you have power.

(3) Take ACTION where you have power.

(4) RELEASE anything over which you don't have power.

(5) Make GRATITUDE a daily habit.

A lot of times we have #Resentment towards individuals, and the problem is we never learn to address our #Resentment. Instead, we tend to hold it in, and we end up paying the price for not releasing our pain.

#Resentment can be extremely difficult to address, but if you're willing to try and release some of that pain and anger, here's another exercise that I used to help me with my #Resentment:

(1) Identify who you have #Resentment towards.

(2) Write that individual a #Resentment letter and express yourself.

(3) Make sure you get it all out! Don't hold back anything. It's your choice to forgive, or not to forgive. This exercise is for you to release your anger and pain.

(4) Take the keys back to your life.

(5) Give it to God...and move on!

RESENTMENT LETTER

Dear John Doe,

I never thought that I would get a chance to express my feelings to you. If this letter ever reaches you, I hope you can at least respect me for being honest and transparent with you. The first thing I want to say to you is that when you murdered my uncle, you change my life forever. Not only did you traumatize me, but you also stole a piece of me. You put my family through hell and because of you we were all left with a permanent scar on our hearts.

I've wiped countless tears from my family members' faces all because of your actions. Many days and nights, I sat and brainstormed how I'd kill you myself. Just thinking about your blood soaked on the pavement and the coroners scraping your body off the ground brought relief to my heart. I was hellbent on seeking revenge! I convinced myself that street justice would be just as acceptable as legal justice.

It might surprise you to know that I think about you all the time. I ask myself, "Is he enjoying life? Does he have kids? Does he feel any guilt or regret about taking my uncle from his only son?"

To be honest with you, you messed me up...but I now understand that it was always me who gave you the power to do so. I let you control my emotions. I let you control my thoughts, and I also let you control my actions.

Today I wrote you this letter to inform you that I'm taking my life back. I have to bury this anger and #Resentment that I've got towards you because I'm the one who is suffering. One Bible verse that I've always believed to be true was, "You will reap what you sow."

This verse is simple. It's saying if you do good then good things will come to you. It concludes with saying if you do bad then you will be punished for your actions. With that verse in mind, it is not my job to judge you, nor punish you for your actions. From this point on, I'm placing everything in God's hands.

P.S. I'm done with it.

FROM ME TO YOU

IF YOU'VE BEEN a victim of rape, child molestation, or child pornography, I encourage you to try this exercise.

If you have a loved one who's been murdered, or if you've been abandoned or betrayed, I encourage you to try this exercise.

Are you a victim of police brutality? Maybe you're a victim of domestic violence, or child abuse? No matter what your #Resententment is, I encourage you to try this exercise and hopefully it will help you like it helped me.

> *Proverbs 24:3-4 | By wisdom a house is built, and by understanding it is established; by knowledge the rooms are filled with all precious pleasant riches.*

YOU ONLY LIVE ONCE

ONE THING that I'm grateful for when it comes to my incarceration is understanding. Being forced to wake up behind a barbed wire fence has given me a lot of time to stop and think about my life.

Many times I've stated that my present term of incarceration is a blessing in disguise. This is because when I was home, death was something that I thought about almost every day. Every morning when I would open my closet door to get dressed, it was hard for me not to notice the twenty-plus "Rest in Peace" t-shirts that I had accumulated over the years. Each t-shirt had a picture with a friend or family member that I had lost, all to gun violence. These murders left me traumatized and resentful and to be honest...I still have mixed emotions towards my uncle's killer.

I constantly ask myself, "Should I turn the other cheek and forgive a man who has spilled my family's blood on the pavement? Or is an eye for an eye the recipe that I'll need to heal my pain and resentment?"

Today, the scale leans more towards me trying to find forgiveness. I've witnessed tears falling from the eyes of many mothers who lost their children to senseless Black on Black gun violence. Even with everything I saw, it's sad to say that the statistics of killing each other has only escalated over the years.

#YouOnlyLiveOnce! With that in mind, upon my release from prison, I plan to distance myself from all the envy, anger, and hatred that plagues the city of Pittsburgh.

Recently, I was watching the fireworks with a couple of inmates on a warm summer night, and the explosion of colors that filled the sky immediately took my mind to another place. I felt like I grew wings because for a moment I felt so free! The vibrations from the fireworks, mixed with the beautiful colors that painted the sky, made my soul feel so alive. I began to daydream and my thoughts drifted towards my family. I said to myself, "I wonder what everyone is doing right now?" That thought instantly snapped me back into reality.

My emotions went from being amused...to feeling cheerless and unhappy. I started stressing about my daughter's birthday, which led me to feel guilty because I knew I'd be absent for a fifth straight year.

Missing out on my children growing up has been my biggest struggle during my incarceration. Even on a regular Monday or Sunday, it kills me not to see their faces. Challenging myself to not feel inadequate has been tough since the day I was federally indicted.

At this point, being back in my children's lives is the only cure for my current pain. Moving forward, I will continue to train myself wholeheartedly to let go of my criminal lifestyle. I came to realize that living life doesn't just consist of breathing air and trying to make it through the day. I believe that living life is finding your purpose and understanding what you were put on this earth to do. Each day, I will continue to follow my intuition, and I will always let my conscience by my guide.

> *Louis Farrakhan | There really can be no peace without justice. There can be no justice without truth. There can be no truth unless someone rises up to tell you the truth.*

PUBLIC SERVICE ANNOUNCEMENT

This is for Black men:

I, Lewis Burt, am here to inform you that the federal justice system is racist and rigged. The judges, the district attorneys, and yes, your own court-appointed lawyer are all in cahoots. If you're a Black man, not only are you faced with this triple threat, but going to trial in federal court is like committing suicide.

If you didn't know, the Department of Justice reported a 93% conviction rate. To break it down: this means you almost never win at trial. You may think paying or hiring your attorney is wise, but I can guarantee you that hiring your own attorney usually pisses the federal government off more.

Their attorneys—the ones appointed by the federal government—are generally useless. I believe the attorneys they hire could care less about you. From my experience, they want you to cooperate as one of their informants, make you a snitch, or convince you to sign a bogus plea deal that you don't deserve. I say, "That you don't deserve," because I've literally witnessed innocent Black men get hundreds upon hundreds of years all because they chose to challenge the federal government at trial versus taking the plea the government offered.

The federal sentencing guidelines are unfair and cruel; the federal sentencing guidelines are systematically designed to enslave Black men. For decades the federal sentencing guidelines have been known to be unjust, but they won't fix the guidelines because the federal government would lose out on billions of dollars. Prisons make billions of dollars! Black men are the majority of what keep prisons full, and up and running. Welcome to legalized slavery.

Here is a list of things that I recommend #BlackMen educate yourselves on, before it's too late:

(1) 18 U.S.C 922(g)

(2) 18 U.S.C 924(c)

(3) 18 U.S.C 924(e)

(4) 851Mandatory Minimum: If the defendant has two such priors, the government can enhance the mandatory minimum to life. (Hence the nickname, Three Strikes Law)

(5) Career Offenders: Persons who commit a crime after two prior felony convictions for those crimes.

CHAPTER 12

THIS IS MY STORY, and it's still being written.
I'm going to start from Chapter 12, so you can see how I was living.

I was in and out of the system; I was trying to play the victim.
Recidivism was chasing me; now I'm a statistic.
I never did listen; my Mom tried to warn me.
She has three sons, and all of us are in prison.

I'm trying to paint a picture so you can feel my pain.
I don't minimize anything. I'm the one to blame.

This is my last chance, so I've gotta get my mind right.
360-to-Life, damn! That doesn't even sound right.

851, Career Criminal.
I will never see the light, no subliminal.

I'm currently in prison.

If I still don't choose to change.
I'll probably end up back in jail, or in the streets...slain.

God shows us signs to follow to our blessings.
This program is one of them, and I'm receptive to his message.

Isaiah 40:31 | But they who wait for the Lord shall renew their strength; they shall mount up with wings like eagles; they shall run and not be weary; they shall walk and not faint.

BROKEN WINGS

ALMOST EVERY MORNING, my alarm clock sounds off at 4:20 a.m. After hitting the snooze button, I drop to my knees, and I always thank God for a new day. After my prayer, I usually find myself on my bunk in deep thought.

My thoughts seem to always drift towards my family, my future, and my freedom. These past five years that I've been incarcerated have allowed me to view life through a whole other lens. I came to understand that even before my present term of incarceration...I was a prisoner. I say that I was a prisoner because I was enslaved to a certain way of thinking. In other words, I was trapped in my own mind.

My thoughts eventually became my choices. My poor choices then led me to become a statistic of the environment. I was a young Black male who chose to drop out of school in the ninth grade only to become a convicted felon.

I'm a statistic of recidivism, and I've also added to the statistic of leaving my children fatherless. Being a contribution to all those categories makes me feel degraded, and ashamed. I feel like a bird with two #BrokenWings, and not being able to fly makes me feel like a failure.

Recently, I went outside in the early morning hours to catch some fresh air, and a morning prayer. After my prayer, I opened my eyes and I was amazed at how beautiful the sky was that morning. The grass seemed to be the perfect shade of green, and the breeze at my back felt just right. It was one of those perfect mornings. I couldn't help but to notice as multiple birds took to the sky and flew freely across the other side of the fence.

As I watched the birds fly to freedom without any resistance, I silently wished that I could fly over the fence myself. I struggle every day with waking up behind these prison walls. Even though my name is Lewis Burt, F.C.I. Fort Dix makes me feel like I'm just number 35321-068.

I will challenge myself first by understanding that just because I'm incarcerated doesn't mean that my inmate number has to define me. I will also challenge myself by demonstrating that it is possible to change for the better even after becoming a statistic of my environment and recidivism.

Moving forward, I will continue to let my light shine through my character. I will take these remaining months of my prison sentence and use this time wisely to help heal my #BrokenWings.

Lastly, when I step foot on the other side of this barbed wire fence, I will spread my wings and take my place in the sky.

> *Lewis Burt III | I believe we all have a purpose. To find it we have to tap into ourselves.*

SELF-MASTERY

FOR MOST OF MY LIFE, I came to realize that I never knew who I was. Looking in the mirror seemed pointless. Even though I saw my reflection, I still wasn't able to identify who Lewis Burt III really was. Like a lost soul, I roamed this earth for years without any sense of purpose or direction.

I was programmed and I did what I thought was required of me to fit into the system of society. I struggled to unlock the true me, denying myself of my own uniqueness. Instead, I was stuck trying to mirror society and I started following the followers. Me following others became another case of the blind leading the blind.

Sometimes punishment can be the eye opener that we need to change. I'm a living testament to that because my current term of incarceration has been one the biggest blessings that I've ever received. I came to believe that a power greater than myself could—and will—restore me back to sanity. By understanding this, I've become more fearless, and these days I think outside the box.

Living in my own truth has been a peaceful experience. Even though I'm being held at F.C.I. Fort Dix, I still feel free. Recently, I came to the conclusion that distance is just an illusion created by my own ordinary assumptions.

What I seek is within my reach.

I still struggle with tapping into my full potential because I allow my cognitions to manipulate and control my mind state.

I've been challenging myself by understanding that self-maintenance is just as important as self-development. Staying focused and constantly changing my thinking patterns has allowed me to follow my intuition. This discipline has opened my mind to a platter full of knowledge and understanding.

Moving forward, I will always let my conscience be my guide. The combination of my conscience and my intuition are the only two things that keep my soul alive.

#SelfMastery can take a lifetime to accomplish. With every breath in my body, I will discover my purpose and leave behind a legacy that can only be labeled as my own.

LEGACY

YOUR PERSONAL #Legacy is more than simply a statement of how you wish to be remembered after you pass on—it is something that enriches your life, reveals you, and discloses what your life is about to your family, friends, and your community.

Ask yourself, what will be my #Legacy?

What mark will you leave on the world?

My name is Lewis Burt III.
I am a Black man.
I am historic.
I do not need a month.
I exist for a lifetime.

EPILOGUE

BARACK OBAMA once said, change will not come if we wait for some other person, or some other time. We are the ones we've been waiting for! We are the change that we seek.

I believe this to be true because I can't save my brothers until I save myself. My pain and disclosure about my life wasn't meant for me to heal alone, but for us to heal together.

> *Martin Luther King, Jr. | Our lives begin to end the day we become silent about things that matter-.*

I pray that my story will give other inmates, convicted felons, and Black men hope about their future. I'm a living testament to the fact that you can break the cycle and change for the better.

> *Kunta Kinte | They can put chains on your body. Never let them put chains on your mind.*

I was able to stay focused and not lose myself mentally. To save myself, I had to be honest with myself. I've made some poor choices in my life. I've done things I'm not proud of, but my poor choices and past failures will not define me as a person.

Nipsey Hussle taught me that the best thing you can do for a person is inspire them. That's the best currency you can offer: inspiration. When a person can rely on you for that, that empowers them in every realm of their life.

Being inspired: it empowers them in their relationships, it empowers them in their business, in their art, and in their creativity. It empowers them because without inspiration, you're dry.

If you're an inmate—with or without a date to return back to society—this is for you.

If you're a convicted felon and you think the odds are stacked against you, then this is for you.

If you're a #BlackMan ...then this is for you.

I'm letting you know that your future is in your hands. The only person who can stop you is you.